live YOUR BEST life

summersdale

An Hachette UK Company
www.hachette.co.uk

Summersdale Publishers Ltd
Part of Octopus Publishing Group Limited
Carmelite House
50 Victoria Embankment
LONDON
EC4Y 0DZ
UK

www.summersdale.com

Printed and bound in China

ISBN: 978-1-78685-751-4

Substantial discounts on bulk quantities of Summersdale books are available to corporations, professional associations and other organizations. For details contact general enquiries: telephone: +44 (0) 1243 771107 or email: enquiries@summersdale.com.

TO:

. . . .

FROM:

. . . .

No act of kindness,
however small, is
ever wasted.

Aesop

Introduction

It's no secret that the best way to be happy is to make others so; when you lift someone up, it lifts you up too! This is the message at the heart of this little book: all you need to live life to the full is an outlook of gratitude and generosity. Tucked away in the everyday are so many moments to enjoy and opportunities to spread kindness — all we need to do is take the time to notice them. So, brighten your world and the world around you, and let this book be your guide to living your best and happiest life.

Spread Kindness

It's always cheering to see a friendly face, so be that person and give someone a smile as you go about your day. Whether you're greeting a colleague, a friend, a shop assistant, or you're just passing someone in the street, smiling is a great way to bring a little sunshine to the day.

He who sows courtesy
reaps friendship, and
he who plants kindness
gathers love.

St Basil

LITTLE THINGS TO ENJOY

The first sip of your morning cuppa

THERE ARE
ALWAYS
FLOWERS FOR
THOSE WHO
WANT TO
SEE THEM.

Henri Matisse

*Happiness,
not in another
place but this
place... not for
another hour,
but this hour.*

Walt Whitman

Spread Kindness

Hold the door open for someone. Whether you hold the door of the lift or let someone into a shop before you, take the time to notice who's around you and be willing to offer a helping hand. It's normal to expect others to put themselves first, so showing a person that you've acknowledged them, even if you don't know them, will brighten their day.

How wonderful it is
that nobody need
wait a single minute
before starting to
improve the world.

Anne Frank

What ARE you LOOKING FORWARD to?

____

Goodness is the only
investment that
never fails.

LITTLE THINGS TO ENJOY

Feeling the sunshine on your face

Remember there's no such thing as a small act of kindness. Every act creates a ripple with no logical end.

Scott Adams

Spread Kindness

If you've had an impressive meal in a restaurant, been on a tour with a great guide, or even just had a good experience with a company's customer service, don't keep it to yourself! Take the time to leave a good review on the company website or on social media to show your appreciation. If you can give a shout-out by name, even better!

This is a
wonderful day.
I've never seen
this one before.

MAYA ANGELOU

LITTLE THINGS TO ENJOY

Sitting down
after being on your
feet all day

The present moment
is filled with joy and
happiness. If you are
attentive, you will see it.

Thích Nhất Hạnh

What
—WAS YOUR—
favourite
moment
of
today?

Spread Kindness

Say thank you! Acknowledge the staff who serve you in a shop, or send a message to a friend or family member to say thank you to them for something they've done for you. It's such a simple act, but it is one of the most powerful things we can do to make the world a kinder and happier place.

If the only prayer
you said in your whole
life was thank you,
that would suffice.

What
GOOD
things
HAVE
HAPPENED
this
week?

IT IS ONLY
WITH
GRATITUDE
THAT LIFE
BECOMES
RICH.

Dietrich Bonhoeffer

LITTLE THINGS
TO ENJOY

Hearing a great
song on the radio

The art of being
happy lies
in the power
of extracting
happiness from
common things.

Henry Ward Beecher

Spread Kindness

Let someone go before you in a queue. It costs only a couple of minutes of your day, but the act of kindness will leave both of you feeling cheered!

The more you praise
and celebrate your
life, the more there is
in life to celebrate.

Oprah Winfrey

LITTLE THINGS TO ENJOY

What HAS made YOU SMILE today?

The problem with
people is they forget
that most of the
time it's the small
things that count.

LITTLE THINGS TO ENJOY

The comfort of
a hot shower

The more you
express gratitude
for what you
have, the more
likely you will
have even more
to express
gratitude for.

Zig Ziglar

What

— HAVE —

you

accomplished

today?

Spread Kindness

If you have a couple of spare coins in your purse, put them in a vending machine as a surprise for the next person who comes along. Even the smallest gift will bring joy to the person who finds it!

Gentleness and kindness
will make our homes a
paradise on earth.

C. A. Bartol

LITTLE THINGS
TO ENJOY

Fresh sheets
on the bed

What

ARE YOU

GLAD

about

today?

Write it
on your heart that
every day is the best
day in the year.

RALPH WALDO EMERSON

Spread Kindness

Reach out to a friend and say hello! You never know what kind of day other people are having, and sending a kind message to a friend to ask them how they're doing could make a real difference and give them the boost they need.

KINDNESS
GIVES
BIRTH TO
KINDNESS.

Sophocles

What MAKES

YOU

FEEL

good?

The power of finding
beauty in the humblest
things makes home
happy and life lovely.

Louisa May Alcott

LITTLE THINGS TO ENJOY

Kind hearts
are the gardens.
Kind thoughts
are the roots.
Kind words are
the blossoms.
Kind deeds are
the fruits.

Kirpal Singh

Spread Kindness

Offer your help whenever you can. It could be with something around the house such as helping with the washing up; you could take on a small extra task at work; or you could help someone carry something heavy up a flight of stairs. Even if they say no, they will always appreciate being asked.

The best way
to cheer yourself up
is to try to cheer
somebody else up.

MARK TWAIN

LITTLE THINGS TO ENJOY

Having the exact change to pay for something

A single act of kindness
throws out roots in
all directions, and
the roots spring up
and make new trees.

Amelia Earhart

What
— ACTS OF —
kindness
— HAVE YOU —
experienced
recently?

The meaning of life
is to find your gift.
The purpose of life
is to give it away.

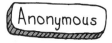

Anonymous

Spread Kindness

If you're out and about and you see litter on the ground, don't ignore it – pick it up and either put it in the bin or recycle it. This small good deed will not only help you do your bit for the community, but you will also be keeping the local wildlife out of danger.

Gratitude is
the memory
of the heart.

JEAN-BAPTISTE MASSIEU

What HAVE YOU LEARNED this week?

What a
wonderful life I've
had! I only wish I'd
realized it sooner.

COLETTE

LITTLE THINGS TO ENJOY

Sharing a joke
with a friend

Your acts of
kindness are
iridescent wings
of divine love,
which linger and
continue to uplift
others long after
your sharing.

Rumi

Spread Kindness

If you have a friend, family member or colleague who is unwell, send them a get-well card. It doesn't have to be fancy, nor do you need to write a long, elaborate message inside - the fact that you've thought of them will be comforting and make them smile.

Feeling gratitude and
not expressing it is like
wrapping a present
and not giving it.

William Arthur Ward

LITTLE THINGS TO ENJOY

Stepping on a crunchy leaf

Don't hurry, don't
worry. And be sure
to smell the flowers
along the way.

Walter Hagen

Whose

FRIENDSHIP

ARE YOU

GRATEFUL

for?

Look for a way
to lift someone up.
And if that's all you
do, that's enough.

ELIZABETH LESSER

Spread Kindness

Offer compliments when you can. If you admire something someone's done, what they've said, or what they're wearing, let them know about it! A kind word does wonders to boost people's spirits, and sharing your warm thoughts will lift you up too.

Which possessions bring you joy?

GRATITUDE IS THE FAIREST BLOSSOM WHICH SPRINGS FROM THE SOUL.

Henry Ward Beecher

LITTLE THINGS
TO ENJOY

When your music
is in time with
your footsteps

I cried because
I had no shoes
until I met
a man who had
no feet.

Persian proverb

Spread Kindness

Raising money for a good cause is a sure-fire way to spread kindness in the world. Use your skills (baking, playing an instrument, interacting with people), or challenge yourself to do something new (skydiving or running a race), and invest some time in making your corner of the world a kinder place.

A KIND AND
COMPASSIONATE
ACT IS OFTEN
ITS OWN
REWARD.

William John Bennett

LITTLE THINGS
TO ENJOY

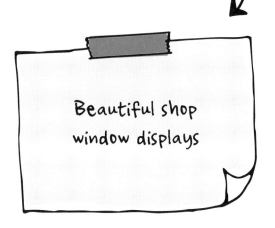

Beautiful shop
window displays

Forever is
composed
of nows.

Emily Dickinson

What DO YOU LOVE ABOUT yourself?

Stop now.
Enjoy the moment.
It's now or never.

MAXIME LAGACE

LITTLE THINGS
TO ENJOY

A new episode
of your favourite
TV show

When
— WERE YOU —
able to help
someone
else?

There are only two
ways to live your life.
One is as though
nothing is a miracle.
The other is as though
everything is a miracle.

Spread Kindness

If you've gone away somewhere, why not bring something back for your close friends or family? Whether it's a small trinket, a postcard or even something you find naturally, such as a beautiful shell from a beach, any gesture to let someone know you're thinking about them will be appreciated.

The fragrance
always stays in the
hand that gives
the rose.

HADA BEJAR

LITTLE THINGS
TO ENJOY

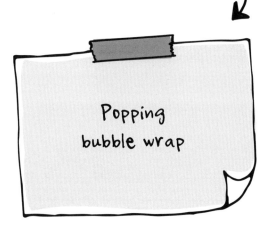

Which
OUTFIT
makes

YOU

FEEL

great?

What sunshine is
to flowers, smiles
are to humanity.

Joseph Addison

Spread Kindness

Remember to say happy birthday! Like many acts of kindness, it's only a small gesture, but the fact that you remembered and cared about making the effort to say it can bring extra cheer to that person's special day.

Joy is what happens to us when we allow ourselves to recognize how good things really are.

Marianne Williamson

LITTLE THINGS TO ENJOY

who
HAS
made
YOU
SMILE
lately?

We can complain
because rose bushes
have thorns, or
rejoice because
thorns have roses.

Jean-Baptiste Alphonse Karr

Spread Kindness

Take time to listen to small talk. It may often seem trivial, but nothing makes people feel more valued than when you remember things they say. Ask about how their weekend camping trip was or how their daughter's exam went - they will be touched that you asked!

The best portion of
a good man's life is
his little, nameless,
unremembered acts of
kindness and of love.

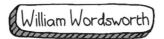

LITTLE THINGS TO ENJOY

Getting green
lights for your
whole journey

Let us be grateful to the people who make us happy; they are the charming gardeners who make our souls blossom.

Marcel Proust

Which opportunities —ARE YOU— grateful for?

Spread Kindness

If you know someone who is going through a hard time, or perhaps you just want to give a friend a nice surprise, send them a small gift or care package in the post. Choose whatever you want - a book, some snacks, a pair of socks, or something that you know will make them laugh. Giving the gift will make both of you feel great.

Seek to do good
and you will find
that happiness will
run after you.

JAMES FREEMAN
CLARKE

What
ARE YOU
GOOD
at?

_ _ _ _ _ _ _ _ _ _ _ _

Sometimes your joy
is the source of your
smile, but sometimes
your smile can be the
source of your joy.

Thich Nhat Hanh

LITTLE THINGS TO ENJOY

Receiving
a package in
the mail

WRITE IT ON
YOUR HEART
THAT EVERY
DAY IS THE
BEST DAY IN
THE YEAR.

Ralph Waldo Emerson

Spread Kindness

Donate your old or unworn clothes to a charity shop. Not only will you be helping someone else by giving away your unwanted things, but clearing space and creating more order in your wardrobe will give you a sense of satisfaction and peace.

LITTLE THINGS TO ENJOY

A long, hot bubble bath

Love one another
and you will be happy.
It's as simple and as
difficult as that.

Michael Leunig

What

— LIFE LESSONS —

are you glad

to have

learned?

How beautiful
a day can be when
kindness touches it!

GEORGE ELLISTON

Spread Kindness

If you've had great service in a restaurant, leave a little extra on top of your tip - even if it's only a few coins. Acknowledging to the staff that you've had a good time and that they've made you feel cared for is sure to put a spring in their step for the rest of their shift.

When I started
counting my blessings,
my whole life
turned around.

WILLIE NELSON

What
ARE
your

FAVOURITE

MEMORIES?

LITTLE THINGS
TO ENJOY

A surprise message
from a friend

Joy comes not through
possession or ownership,
but through a wise
and loving heart.

Buddhist proverb

Spread Kindness

Send an encouraging message to someone. Perhaps a colleague has an important presentation to give – send an email to wish them luck. Maybe a friend has organized an event for the group – reach out to say thank you for their efforts. Supporting the people around you is a great way to strengthen your bonds with others, and everybody will be happier as a result.

LITTLE THINGS TO ENJOY

Completing a
to-do list

Great
opportunities to
help others seldom
come, but small
ones surround
us every day.

Sally Koch

What

— IS THE MOST —

beautiful

thing you

have seen

today?

Spread Kindness

Many supermarkets have donation boxes, so next time you go shopping, consider buying an extra tin of beans, a can of soup or a couple of toothbrushes to donate to your local food bank.

WHEREVER
THERE IS A
HUMAN BEING,
THERE IS AN
OPPORTUNITY
FOR KINDNESS.

Seneca

What do you LOVE ABOUT YOUR life?

LITTLE THINGS TO ENJOY

A hug from
a loved one

Spread Kindness

If you have the opportunity, buy locally or use independent shops rather than buying from a chain store. Whether you're buying clothes or fruit and veg, taking the time to support local businesses is a great way to help the community, and your custom will be appreciated.

Genuine kindness is
no ordinary act, but a
gift of rare beauty.

SYLVIA ROSSETTI

LITTLE THINGS TO ENJOY

The smell of the air after it's rained

What —EXPERIENCES— are you grateful for?

Everyone wants to live
on top of the mountain,
but all the happiness
and growth occurs while
you're climbing it.

Andy Rooney

Spread Kindness

Give others your time, however
you can. Perhaps someone at
work needs help with a task, or
your friend needs a lift somewhere.
Maybe you could even consider
volunteering regularly for a cause
you feel strongly about. However
you choose to donate your time,
you will be spreading kindness in
the world.

What **HAVE** you

IMPROVED at

recently?

The secrets of
happiness lie in
our capacity
to expand
our heart.

Amit Ray

LITTLE THINGS
TO ENJOY

Having your
favourite food
for dinner

What
— WAS YOUR —
favourite
holiday?

Kindness is a
language which the
deaf can hear and
the blind can see.

Christian Nestell Bovee

LITTLE THINGS
TO ENJOY

Waking up
and realizing it's
the weekend

Spread Kindness

Next time you see someone fundraising – whether it's an email sent round at work or a post on social media – consider donating. Even a small amount will be appreciated by the fundraiser and will help towards their goal. If you're unable to donate, help them to spread the message by telling others.

We make a
living by what we get,
but we make a life
by what we give.

Anonymous

Which —RELATIONSHIPS— make your life richer?

How far that
little candle
throws his beams!
So shines a
good deed in a
naughty world.

William Shakespeare

LITTLE THINGS TO ENJOY

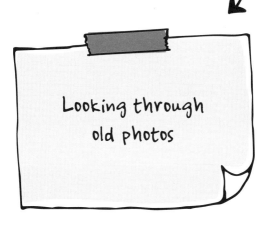

Looking through old photos

IF YOU WANT TO BE A REBEL, BE KIND.

Pancho Ramos Stierle

Spread Kindness

Give people the benefit of the doubt and try not to jump to conclusions. This kindness may not always be felt by others immediately, but interacting with people and thinking of them without judgement will make them feel welcome and both of you will be more comfortable.

A smile is
happiness you'll
find right under
your nose.

TOM WILSON

LITTLE THINGS TO ENJOY

Getting a good
parking space or
seat on the bus

Do your little bit of
good where you are;
it's those little bits of
good put together that
overwhelm the world.

Where

— IS YOUR —

favourite

place

to be?

No matter
how dark things
seem to be or
actually are, raise
your sights and see
possibilities – always
see them, for they're
always there.

Norman Vincent Peale

Spread Kindness

Leave encouraging sticky notes for people to find. Around the house, slipped into a friend's bag, on the noticeboard at work, inside a library book - wherever you leave little messages of positivity you're sure to spark some joy.

Reflect upon your present blessings – of which every man has plenty – not on your past misfortunes, of which all men have some.

Charles Dickens

What MADE you

LAUGH

most

recently?

Do unto others as you would have them do unto you.

LUKE 6:31

LITTLE THINGS TO ENJOY

The cool side
of the pillow

Those who bring
sunshine to the lives
of others cannot keep
it from themselves.

J. M. Barrie

Spread Kindness

Nothing bonds people and brings them closer together quite like sharing a bite to eat, so next time you have a packet of something, offer it around. You never know what conversations it could spark, or whose day you might be brightening with this little act of kindness.

LITTLE THINGS
TO ENJOY

One of the most
difficult things
to give away
is kindness; it
usually comes
back to you.

Anonymous

Who
HAS
helped
YOU TO
SOLVE
a
problem?

Compassion is the
greatest form of love
humans have to offer.

Rachael Joy Scott

Spread Kindness

Introduce people to each other. Perhaps a friend is looking for someone to help them with a project, or a work colleague is looking for a mentor or someone with a particular skill. Offer to be the connecting link and put people in touch with each other.

One joy dispels a
hundred cares.

CONFUCIUS

LITTLE THINGS TO ENJOY

BE HAPPY
FOR THIS
MOMENT.
THIS MOMENT
IS YOUR LIFE.

Omar Khayyam

What
—DO YOU WANT—
to thank
yourself
for?

It is not how much
we have, but how
much we enjoy, that
makes happiness.

Charles Spurgeon

If you're interested in finding out more about our books, find us on Facebook at Summersdale Publishers and follow us on Twitter at @Summersdale.

www.summersdale.com